A SOLDIER'S STRENGTH FROM THE PSALMS

JOURNAL AND COUNTDOWN CALENDAR

By Sharon L. Patterson
Illustrated by Carrie Allison

Sharon L. Patterson
A SCRIBE FOR ALL SEASONS

Requests for permission to make copies of any part of this work should be emailed to the publisher A Scribe for All Seasons: ascribeforallseasons@gmail.com.

ISBN: 978-1535429467

Printed in the United States of America by CreateSpace

Library of Congress Control Number: 2007900615

FROM THE AUTHOR...

I am both a soldier's mother and a retired soldier's wife. How I understand the uniqueness of your courageous spirit and the sacrificial call to serve your country.

Desiring to be an encourager, I expanded an idea I had for my son during the last months of his tour of duty in Iraq. The result is this journal and countdown calendar filled with strengthening scripture, encouraging words, and portions from actual e-mails sent during my son's deployment.

Knowing that no one comprehends your challenges like another soldier, I looked to one known throughout time. He righteously protected the innocent; stood firm on the ferocious frontlines of battle; patrolled dangerous checkpoints; walked the lonely late-night and early-morning watches; guarded the city gates; climbed rugged terrain in all kinds of weather; and faced and chased enemies in the desert and on the mountains.

That soldier, King David, not only endured many of the same things as each of you, but he also needed and drew strength daily from Almighty God. He wrote of his struggles and recorded his prayers and praises, victories, and highs and lows. What encouragement, hope, and comfort come from the Psalms he left to us.

May God be with you and bless, protect, comfort, and lift your spirit daily as you record your own stories of faith on the pages that follow....

With love, prayer, and gratitude for your service,

Sharon L. Patterson

HOOAHS!
(Acknowledgments)

PHOTOGRAPHS

Courtesy of the Armed Service's Public Domain, with credit given to contributing photographers; private photo collection of SGT David J. Milliman.

ILLUSTRATIONS

Carrie Allison

CALENDAR LAYOUT (ORIGINAL DESIGN)

Garry Patterson

JOURNAL (ORIGINAL DESIGN)

Sharon L. Patterson

WORDS OF ENCOURAGEMENT

From released e-mails from Chaplain Craig Combs, e-mails to Sergeant David J. Milliman from Sharon L. Patterson, Colonel (Ret) Garry D. Patterson, and a letter from Joshua, written by Janis East.

SCRIPTURE SOURCE

The Psalms taken from the New International Version of the Bible. All scripture quotations, unless otherwise indicated, are taken from the HOLY BIBLE, NEW INTERNATIONAL VERSION®. NIV®. Copyright ©1973, 1978, 1984 by International Bible Society. Used by permission of Zondervan. All rights reserved.

INSPIRATIONAL SOURCE

The spirit and sacrifice of all you Courageous Ones who serve in our Armed Forces everywhere!!!

"HOOAHS"

The first time I attended a military function and heard the word "hooah" shouted by an officer to his troops followed by the resounding "hooah" echoed back by his soldiers, I knew it was one powerful zinger of a word. It is an all-encompassing expression full of a "yes" attitude; a "let's do it" mentality; and an inexhaustable source of positive encouragement. Every time I hear it, the same feeling rolls over me, as if it were the very first time.

Every soldier understands it even though each branch of service has a slight variation of the word. It has the same effect no matter the small difference in sound.

Over twenty centuries ago, when the world was under the domination of the Roman Empire, a great encourager of the early Christian churches began to write letters to inspire them to stand up under intense persecution and even possible death. One of my favorite verses penned by that great inspirer, the apostle Paul, is found in Philippians 4:8: "Finally, brothers, whatever is true, whatever is noble, whatever is right, whatever is pure, whatever is lovely, whatever is admirable—if anything is excellent or praiseworthy—think about such things."

If he were here today, I'm not sure this strong soldier of Christ might not end that verse with "hooah"! It is my prayer that there will be many times each of you opens this journal and finds true, right, pure, lovely, and admirable pieces of inspiration and encouragement that causes your very soul to hear "hooahs" from God, our Commander-in-Chief!

A NOTE TO THE FAMILIES OF OUR SOLDIERS...

Between March 18, 2004, and March 19, 2005, the keys of my computer and the links to my e-mail stayed hot. Every day possible, I sent messages, prayers, and words of encouragement to my son stationed inside the Green Zone in Baghdad, Iraq. Many times, I received encouragement back from my son through the stories he shared with me.

There were nondescript bits of information from home and sometimes there were moments my heart came out through my fingers, trying to touch the soul of my son in harm's way. There were sentence prayers and long paragraph prayers, but always there was prayer.

It was a long year, filled with anxious moments, lonesome holidays, and the anticipation of my son's homecoming. There were blessed times, fearful hours, funny instances, and unexpected moments of joy. It was some kind of journey. I knew that I wanted to share that journey with other soldiers and their families about midway through my son's deployment. However, I had to wait until the emotions we had to process and the faith journey we experienced came into full rear mirror view.

Our son is a purple-heart recipient and the inspiration for this journal/countdown calendar. So are your sons and daughters!

God bless you one and all!

Sharon L. Patterson

WORDS OF ENCOURAGEMENT

(from an e-mail from my husband, Colonel (Ret) Garry Patterson to our son)

Good morning! It is Friday morning and I was thinking of you. I pray that you are doing well physically, mentally, and spiritually. You make us so proud to call you son. Our country is in debt to you and the other men and women like you who are making such great sacrifices for freedom. This morning your mother and I prayed a prayer of protection and blessing on you. I know that the good Lord is watching over you and giving you peace in troubled times.

I know that when I was deployed, that my faith was even more important to me than I could ever have imagined. I hope that you will continue to grow in your faith and knowledge of the Lord. I feel truly thankful to have a son such as you. I also look forward to the day that you and your fellow soldiers return to Ft. Hood and your loved ones. It will be a magnificent celebration of a job well done and be a time for rejoicing.

I know that it appears to be a long way off, but will come faster than you can really imagine. You are going to hit a mental wall during your deployment. I know, because I also did. It usually happens a little after the half way point. For me, it only lasted a couple of weeks and then I got my second wind. During this time, it is important to stay busy and both physically and mentally to continue on and stay alert. Before you know it, your unit will begin making the initial plans for redeployment home. I pray that you will be strengthened and blessed by our prayers and that you will always know that we love you and cherish you so very much.

Take care and as always, be safe!

JANUARY

Bible Update Brief

1

Psalm 5: 11: "But let all who take refuge in you be glad; let them ever sing for joy. Spread your protection over them, that those who love your name may rejoice in you."

2

Psalm 1: 6: "For the Lord watches over the way of the righteous, but the way of the wicked will perish."

3

Psalm 55: 1-3: "Listen to my prayer, O God, do not ignore my plea; hear me and answer me. My thoughts trouble me and I am distraught at the voice of the enemy, at the stares of the wicked."

4

Psalm 90: 14: "Satisfy us in the morning with your unfailing love, that we may sing for joy and be glad all our days."

5

Psalm 112: 8: "His heart is secure, he will have no fear; in the end he will look triumph on his foes."

6

Psalm 23: 5: "You prepare a table before me in the presence of my enemies. You annoint my head with oil, my cup overflows."

7

Psalm 144: 1: "Praise be to the Lord my Rock; who trains my hands for war, my fingers for battle."

JANUARY

After Action Report (AAR)

1

Countdown
DAY

2

Countdown
DAY

3

Countdown
DAY

4

Countdown
DAY

5

Countdown
DAY

6

Countdown
DAY

7

Countdown
DAY

JANUARY

Bible Update Brief

8

Psalm 145: 19: "He fulfills the desires of those who fear Him; he hears their cry and saves them."

9

Psalm 24: 8: "Who is the King of Glory? The Lord strong and mighty, the Lord mighty in battle."

10

Psalm 37: 1-2: "Do not fret because of evil men or be envious of those who do wrong; for like the grass they will soon wither, like green plants they will soon die away."

11

Psalm 140: 1-2: "Rescue me, O Lord, from evil men; protect me from men of violence who devise evil plans in their hearts and stir up war every day."

12

Psalm 145: 13b: "The Lord is faithful to all His promises and loving toward all He has made."

13

Psalm 119: 105: "Your word is a lamp to my feet and a light for my path."

14

Psalm 71: 5: "For you have been my hope, O Sovereign Lord, my confidence since my youth."

JANUARY

After Action Report (AAR)

8

Countdown
DAY

9

Countdown
DAY

10

Countdown
DAY

11

Countdown
DAY

12

Countdown
DAY

13

Countdown
DAY

14

Countdown
DAY

JANUARY

Bible Update Brief

15

Psalm 138: 3: "When I called, you answered me; you made me bold and stouthearted."

16

Psalm 25: 20: "Guard my life and rescue me; let me not be put to shame, for I take refuge in you."

17

Psalm 144: 7-8: "Reach down your hand from on high; deliver me and rescue me from the mighty waters, from the hands of foreigners whose mouths are full of lies, whose right hands are deceitful."

18

Psalm 139: 1-2: "O Lord, you have search me and you know me. You know when I sit down and when I rise; you perceive my thoughts from afar."

19

Psalm 5: 3: "In the morning, O Lord, you hear my voice; in the morning I lay my requests before you and wait in expectation."

20

Psalm 54: 6b-7: "I will praise your name, O Lord, for it is good. For He has delivered me from all my troubles, and my eyes have looked in triumph on my foes."

21

Psalm 3: 1, 3: "O Lord, how many are my foes! How many rise up against me!... But you are a shield around me, O Lord; you bestow glory on me and lift up my head."

JANUARY

After Action Report (AAR)

15

Countdown
DAY

16

Countdown
DAY

17

Countdown
DAY

18

Countdown
DAY

19

Countdown
DAY

20

Countdown
DAY

21

Countdown
DAY

JANUARY

Bible Update Brief

22

Psalm 37: 3: "Trust in the Lord and do good; dwell in the land, and enjoy safe pasture."

23

Psalm 139: 11-12: "If they say, 'Surely the darkness will hide me and the light become night around me,' even the darkenss will not be dark to you; the night will shine like the day, for darkness is as light to you."

24

Psalm 94: 19: "When anxiety was great within me, your consolation brought joy to my soul."

25

Psalm 37: 39: "The salvation of the righteous comes from the Lord; He is their stronghold in time of trouble."

26

Psalm 145: 8: "The lord is gracious and compassionate, slow to anger and rich in love."

27

Psalm 41: 1: "Blessed is he who has regard for the weak; the Lord delivers him in times of trouble."

28

Psalm 71: 3: "Be my rock of refuge to which I can always go; give the command to save me, for you are my rock and my fortess."

JANUARY

After Action Report (AAR)

22

Countdown
DAY

23

Countdown
DAY

24

Countdown
DAY

25

Countdown
DAY

26

Countdown
DAY

27

Countdown
DAY

28

Countdown
DAY

JANUARY

Bible Update Brief

29

Psalm 3: 6: "I will not fear the tens of thousands drawn up against me on every side."

30

Psalm 34: 12: "Whoever of you loves life and desires to see many good days, keep your tongue from evil and your lips from speaking lies."

31

Psalm 84: 12: "O Lord Almighty, blessed is the man who trusts in you."

JANUARY

After Action Report (AAR)

29

Countdown
DAY

30

Countdown
DAY

31

Countdown
DAY

NOTES

Psalm 139:7-8:A

"Where can I go from your Spirit? Where can I flee from your presence?
If I go up to the heavens, you are there."

WORDS OF ENCOURAGEMENT

(from an e-mail dated January 5, 2005)

Good morning Son,

Once again I was delighted by the surprise of hearing your voice in person in the middle of the day. I told you it literally makes my heart surge!!! Your son loved listening to "Daddy" on the phone. I have heard him say "bye" but never "bye, Daddy" before. It seems you rate pretty high, getting many of the "firsts" even though you are not here. I couldn't be more pleased that it happened on the phone to you.

I was sorry to hear about the losses yesterday. God be with all of you today. These are hard days, I know. It makes me want to pray more diligently, to stay on the wall and to pray for defeat at every turn for the enemy.

May their weapons miss their marks, misfire, and explode before they reach their targets. May their holes of hiding be uncovered, may they find no rest. May they turn on one another; may their courage be turned to running cowardice....

May our eyes be sharper, our bravery greater, our weapons more lethal, our strength and resolve more powerful...our cause purer, our determination steadier.

I love you, brave son. Keep on keeping on. You are on the side of righteousness and freedom's light. Never lose sight of that for a moment. You are so precious to me.

Love and prayers for Divine intervention and great peace in the battle's heat,

Mom

FEBRUARY

Bible Update Brief

1

Psalm 98: 8-9: "Let the rivers clap their hands, let the mountains sing together for joy; let them sing before the Lord, for He comes to judge the earth. He will judge the world in righteousness and the peoples with equity."

2

Psalm 119: 107: "I have suffered much; preserve my life, O Lord, according to your word."

3

Psalm 33: 10-11: "The Lord foils the plans of the nations, He thwarts the purposes of the peoples. But the plans of the Lord stand from forever, the purposes of His heart through all generations."

4

Psalm 112: 7: "He will have no fear of bad news; his heart is steadfast, trusting in the Lord."

5

Psalm 40: 11: "Do not withheld your mercy from me, O Lord; may your love and your truth always protect me."

6

Psalm 103: 11: "For as high as the heavens are above the earth, so great is His love for those who fear him."

7

Psalm 117: 2: "For great is His love toward us, and the faithfulness of the Lord endures forever."

FEBRUARY

After Action Report (AAR)

1

Countdown
DAY

2

Countdown
DAY

3

Countdown
DAY

4

Countdown
DAY

5

Countdown
DAY

6

Countdown
DAY

7

Countdown
DAY

FEBRUARY

Bible Update Brief

8

Psalm 142: 1-2: "I cry aloud to the Lord; I lift up my voice to the Lord for mercy. I pour out my complaint before Him; before Him I tell my trouble."

9

Psalm 136: 23-24: "To the One who remembered us in our low estate. His love endures forever. And freed us from our enemies. His love endures forever."

10

Psalm 33: 21: "In Him our hearts rejoice, for we trust in His holy name."

11

Psalm 121: 7: "The Lord will keep you from all harm, He will watch over your life."

12

LINCOLN'S BD

Psalm 37: 28: "For the Lord loves the just and will not forsake his faithful ones."

13

Psalm 56: 13: "For you have delivered me from death and my feet from stumbling that I may walk before God in the light of life."

14

VALENTINE'S DAY

Psalm 143: 9: "Rescue me from my enemies, O Lord, for I hide myself in you."

FEBRUARY

After Action Report (AAR)

8

Countdown
DAY

9

Countdown
DAY

10

Countdown
DAY

11

Countdown
DAY

12

Countdown
DAY

13

Countdown
DAY

14

Countdown
DAY

FEBRUARY

Bible Update Brief

15

Psalm 111: 3: "Glorious and majestic are His deeds, and His righteousness endures forever."

16

Psalm 105: 4: "Look to the Lord and His strength; seek His face always."

17

Psalm 35: 2: "Take up shield and buckler; arise and come to my aid."

18

Psalm 62: 7: "My salvation and my honor depend on God; He is my mighty rock, my refuge."

19

Psalm 119: 116: "Sustain me, according to your promise, and I will live; do not let my hopes be dashed."

20

Psalm 141: 8: "But my eyes are fixed on you, O Sovereign Lord; in you I take refuge-do not give me over to death."

21

WASHINGTON'S BD
PRESIDENT'S DAY
Psalm 72: 14a: "He will rescue them from oppression and violence..."

FEBRUARY

After Action Report (AAR)

15

Countdown
DAY

16

Countdown
DAY

17

Countdown
DAY

18

Countdown
DAY

19

Countdown
DAY

20

Countdown
DAY

21

Countdown
DAY

FEBRUARY

Bible Update Brief

22

Psalm 141: 9-10: "Keep me from the snares they have laid for me, from the traps set by evildoers. Let the wicked fall into their own nets, while I pass by in safety."

23

Psalm 138: 7: "Through I walk in the midst of trouble, you preserve my life; you stretch out your hand against the anger of my foes, with your right hand you save me."

24

Psalm 37: 18: "The days of the blameless are known to the Lord, and their inheritance will endure forever."

25

Psalm 144: 2: "He is my loving God and my fortress, my stronghold and my deliverer, my shield in whom I take refuge..."

26

Psalm 9: 10: "Those who know your name will trust in you, for you, Lord, have never forsaken those who seek you."

27

Psalm 119: 165: "Great peace have they who love your law, and nothing can make them stumble."

28

Psalm 63: 6: "On my bed I remember you; I think of you through the watches of the night."

FEBRUARY

After Action Report (AAR)

22

Countdown
DAY

23

Countdown
DAY

24

Countdown
DAY

25

Countdown
DAY

26

Countdown
DAY

27

Countdown
DAY

28

Countdown
DAY

FEBRUARY

Bible Update Brief

Psalm 35: 1: "Contend, O Lord, with those who contend with me; fight against those who fight against me."

FEBRUARY

After Action Report (AAR)

29

NOTES

NOTES

NOTES

WORDS OF ENCOURAGEMENT

(from an e-mail to my son, July 7, 2004)

Just because you are my son
Just because you are unique in all the world,
Just because you make my heart happy,
Just because you are a miracle from God,
Just because you are a thoughtful son,
Just because you are caring,
Just because you are creative,
Just because you are strong in spirit,
Just because you make a difference in my life,
Just because you are courageous,
Just because you are humorous,
Just because you are a good friend,
Just because you love your son,
Just because you attempt hard things,
Just because you are an incredible soldier,
Just because you have turned weakness into strengths,
Just because you love Jesus,
Just because you once brought me roses, riding your bicycle
Across the railroad tracks,
Just because you sent flowers from Iraq on Mother's Day,
Just because you remember,
Just because you are a good man,
Just because you are you,
Just because you are mine!

Please read this, substituting your own qualities and special remembrances; and know that although this was written to my son, the sentiments are sent to each one of you sons and daughters with pride and greatest blessings!

Sharon L. Patterson

MARCH

Bible Update Brief

1

Psalm 20: 7: "Some trust in chariots and some in horses, but we trust in the name of the Lord our God."

2

Psalm 86: 16a: "Turn to me and have mercy on me; grant your strength to your servant..."

3

Psalm 94: 18: "When I said, 'My foot is slipping,' your love, O Lord, supported me."

4

Psalm 97: 10: "Let those who love the Lord hate evil, for He guards the lives of His faithful ones and delivers them from the hand of the wicked."

5

Psalm 139: 23-24: "Search me, O God, and know my heart; test me and know my anxious thoughts. See if there is any offensive way in me, and lead me in the way everlasting."

6

Psalm 4: 6: "Many are asking, 'Who can show us any good?' Let the light of your face shine upon us, O Lord."

7

Psalm 42: 8: "By the day the Lord directs His love, at night His song is within me-a prayer to the God of my life."

MARCH

After Action Report (AAR)

1

Countdown
DAY

2

Countdown
DAY

3

Countdown
DAY

4

Countdown
DAY

5

Countdown
DAY

6

Countdown
DAY

7

Countdown
DAY

MARCH

Bible Update Brief

8

Psalm 103: 2-3: "Praise the Lord, O my soul, and forget not all His benefits-who forgives all your sins and heals all your diseases."

9

Psalm 71: 14: "But as for me, I will always have hope; I will praise you more and more."

10

Psalm 20: 6: "Now I know that the Lord saves His anointed; He answers from His holy heaven with the saving power of His right hand."

11

Psalm 147: 3: "He heals the brokenhearted and binds up their wounds."

12

Psalm 143: 11: "For your name's sake, O Lord, preserve my life; in your righteousness, bring me out of trouble."

13

Psalm 118: 14: "The Lord is my strength and my song; He has become my salvation."

14

Psalm 95: 2: "Let us come before Him with thanksgiving and extol Him with music and song."

MARCH

After Action Report (AAR)

8

Countdown
DAY

9

Countdown
DAY

10

Countdown
DAY

11

Countdown
DAY

12

Countdown
DAY

13

Countdown
DAY

14

Countdown
DAY

MARCH

Bible Update Brief

15

Psalm 111: 2: "Great are the works of the Lord, they are pondered by all who delight in Him."

16

Psalm 107: 43: "Whoever is wise, let him heed these things and consider the great love of the Lord."

17

Psalm 25: 3: "No one whose hope is in you will ever be put to shame, but they will be put to shame who are treacherous without excuse."

18

Psalm 115: 11: "You who fear Him trust in the Lord-He is their help and shield."

19

Psalm 66: 19: "But God has surely listened and heard my voice in prayer."

20

Psalm 103: 6: "The Lord works righteousness and justice for all the oppressed."

21

Psalm 32: 7: "You are my hiding place; you will protect me from trouble and surround me with songs of deliverance."

MARCH

After Action Report (AAR)

15

Countdown
DAY

16

Countdown
DAY

17

Countdown
DAY

18

Countdown
DAY

19

Countdown
DAY

20

Countdown
DAY

21

Countdown
DAY

MARCH

Bible Update Brief

22

Psalm 36: 9: "For with you is the fountain of life; in your light we see light."

23

Psalm 124: 7: "We have escaped like a bird out of the fowler's snare; the snare has been broken, and we have escaped."

24

Psalm 113: 3: "From the rising of the sun to the place where it sets, the name of the Lord is to be praised."

25

Psalm 109: 21: "But you, O Sovereign Lord, deal well with me for your name's sake; out of the goodness of your love, deliver me."

26

Psalm 109: 27: "Let them know that it is your hand, that you, O Lord, have done it."

27

Psalm 91: 5-6: "You will not fear the terror of night, nor the arrow that flies by day, nor the pestilence that stalks in the darkness, nor the plague that destroys at midday."

28

Psalm 7: 9: "O righteous God, who searches minds and hearts, bring to an end the violence of the wicked and make the righteous secure."

MARCH

After Action Report (AAR)

22

Countdown
DAY

23

Countdown
DAY

24

Countdown
DAY

25

Countdown
DAY

26

Countdown
DAY

27

Countdown
DAY

28

Countdown
DAY

29

    Psalm 71: 21: "You will increase my honor and comfort me once again."

30

    Psalm 89: 13: "Your arm is endued with power; your hand is strong, your right hand exalted."

31

    Psalm 70: 1: "Hasten, O God, to save me; O Lord, come quickly to help me."

MARCH

After Action Report (AAR)

29

Countdown
DAY

30

Countdown
DAY

31

Countdown
DAY

NOTES

NOTES

NOTES

WORDS OF ENCOURAGEMENT

(from Chaplain's BUB #25, Craig Combs, author, on August 19, 2005)

…About 150 meters after driving under an overpass, it happened. We heard a loud explosion and the back of our Hummer flew up and then back down and our cab was immediately filled with dust…we had been hit by an IED (Improvised Explosive Device)….

Everybody did what we were trained to do and we continued on…until we were out of the danger zone. We immediately got out to assess the damage….

As Paul Harvey would say, "Now, for the rest of the story." When we all realized what had just happened and saw that no one was injured, that there wasn't even a scratch on our vehicle, every one of the men, not just their chaplain, began praising and thanking God for His incredible and obvious answer to our prayers of protection. It could not have been any more obvious. It was so unbelievable, after seeing the blast site later. I was even trying to understand it out loud, saying, "Maybe this happened or that happened for the charge to miss us." My men stopped me and said, "Chaplain, forget trying to figure it out or explain it. It's obvious. God protected us with His angels!" 'Nough said. My men were now preaching to me instead of me preaching to them….

Some of the men have tried to insinuate that I personally or my own prayers were the reasons we were not harmed. But when they do, I correct them and point out that it didn't happen because I am a chaplain or some spiritual giant. It can and does happen to anyone who loves God and acknowledges and calls upon His name. It is not my prayers alone, but prayers of countless others who were praying.

APRIL

Bible Update Brief

1

Psalm 143: 12: "In your unfailing love, silence my enemies; destroy all my foes, for I am your servant."

2

Psalm 147: 11: "The Lord delights in those who fear Him, who put their hope in His unfailing love."

3

Psalm 109: 26: "Help me, O Lord my God; save me in accordance with your love."

4

Psalm 37: 5-6: "Commit your way to the Lord; trust in Him and He will do this: He will make your righteousness shine like the dawn, the justice of your cause like the noonday sun."

5

Psalm 104: 1: "Praise the Lord, O my soul. O Lord my God, you are very great; you are clothed with splendor and majesty."

6

Psalm 146: 9: "The Lord watches over the alien and sustains the fatherless and the widow, but He frustrates the way of the wicked."

7

Psalm 27: 13: "I am still confident of this: I will see the goodness of the Lord in the land of the living."

APRIL

After Action Report (AAR)

1

2

3

4

5

6

7

APRIL

Bible Update Brief

8

Psalm 115: 12a, 13: "The Lord remembers us and will bless us...He will bless those who fear the Lord-small and great alike."

9

Psalm 71: 6: "From birth I have relied on you; you brought me forth from my mother's womb."

10

Psalm 34: 4: "I sought the Lord, and He answered me; He delivered me from all my fears."

11

Psalm 37: 39: "The salvation of the righteous comes from the Lord; He is their stronghold in times of trouble."

12

Psalm 124: 2-3: "If the Lord had not been on our side when men attacked us, when their anger flared against us, they would have swallowed us alive."

13

Psalm 89: 21: "My hand will sustain him; surely my arm will strengthen him."

14

Psalm 45: 4: "In your majesty ride forth victoriously in behalf of truth, humility and righteousness; let your hand display awesome deeds."

APRIL

After Action Report (AAR)

8

Countdown
DAY

9

Countdown
DAY

10

Countdown
DAY

11

Countdown
DAY

12

Countdown
DAY

13

Countdown
DAY

14

Countdown
DAY

APRIL

Bible Update Brief

15

Psalm 41: 2: "The Lord will protect him and preserve his life; He will bless him in the land and not surrender him to the desires of the foes."

16

Psalm 66: 16: "Come and listen all you who fear God; let me tell you what he has done for me."

17

Psalm 27: 2: "When evil men advance against me to devour my flesh, when my enemies and my foes attack me, they will stumble and fall."

18

Psalm 57: 3: "He sends from heaven and saves me, rebuking those who hotly pursue me; God sends his love and his faithfulness."

19

Psalm 62: 5: "Find rest, O my soul, in God alone; my hope comes from Him."

20

Psalm 38: 21: "O Lord, do not forsake me; be not far from me, O my God."

21

Psalm 95: 6-7: "Come, let us bow down in worship, let us kneel before the Lord our Maker; for He is our God, and we are the people of His pasture, the flock under His care."

APRIL

After Action Report (AAR)

15

Countdown
DAY

16

Countdown
DAY

17

Countdown
DAY

18

Countdown
DAY

19

Countdown
DAY

20

Countdown
DAY

21

Countdown
DAY

APRIL

Bible Update Brief

22

Psalm 145: 2: "Every day I will praise you and extol your name for ever and ever."

23

Psalm 100: 5: "For the Lord is good and His love endures forever, His faithfulness continues through all generations."

24

Psalm 37: 10-11: "A little while, and the wicked will be no more; though you look for them, they will not be found. But the meek will inherit the land and enjoy great peace."

25

Psalm 143: 10: "Teach me to do your will, for you are my God; may your good Spirit lead me on level ground."

26

Psalm 119: 149: "Hear my voice in accordance with your love; preserve my life, O lord, according to your laws."

27

Psalm 9: 3: "My enemies turn back; they stumble and perish before you."

28

Psalm 86: 17: "Give me a sign of your goodness, that my enemies may see it and be put to shame, for you, O Lord, have helped me and comforted me."

APRIL

After Action Report (AAR)

22

Countdown
DAY

23

Countdown
DAY

24

Countdown
DAY

25

Countdown
DAY

26

Countdown
DAY

27

Countdown
DAY

28

Countdown
DAY

APRIL

Bible Update Brief

29

Psalm 27: 14: "Wait for the Lord; be strong and take heart..."

30

Psalm 34: 15: "The eyes of the Lord are on the righteous and His ears attentive to their cry."

APRIL

After Action Report (AAR)

29

30

NOTES

NOTES

NOTES

WORDS OF ENCOURAGEMENT

(from a letter written for a Father's Day contest by Janis East on behalf
of our son's little boy, Joshua)

My daddy is far, far away in a place called Baghdad. I am just a little boy now, but by the time my daddy gets home I will be two years old.

I miss my daddy a whole lot. Whenever my mommy or my gammy or my grannah or my pawpaw shows me his picture, I say, "DaDa, DaDa!" and blow him kisses. They show me his pictures all the time so I won't forget what he looks like or forget how much he loves me! They also read to me from an e-mail he sent just for me that tells me how much he loves me!

I know my daddy loves me very much because he volunteered to go far away to a very hot, dry place to fight a different type of war. My daddy says he is really lucky to even get to sleep for four whole hours at a time and eat something called MREs. Everyone says it is a war on terror. All I know is that my daddy is doing all that he can to keep me and all the other children in the world a lot safer.

My daddy isn't here, so he can't go eat at a nice restaurant or even eat a hot meal, but I still think my daddy is the best daddy. My daddy loves me enough that he is risking his life every day to keep me safer. My daddy is Jeremy Milliman and he is a soldier in the 1st Cavalry and he is very brave!

Joshua Lane Milliman
18 months old

Special Note: Joshua's letter, written by his grandmother, won him a very special teddy bear for himself and a restaurant gift certificate for his daddy, which he used when he came home on R&R. The letter was read on the air by the radio station Oldies 103.5 for their Father's Day contest in June 2004.

MAY

1

Psalm 139: 9-10: "If I rise on the wings of the dawn, if I settle on the far side of the sea, even there your hand will guide me and your right hand will hold me fast."

2

Psalm 34: 6: "This poor man called, and the Lord heard him; he saved him out of all his troubles."

3

Psalm 107: 20: "He sent forth His word and healed them; he rescued them from the grave."

4

Psalm 86: 15: "But you, O Lord, are a compassionate and gracious God, slow to anger, abounding in love and faithfulness."

5

Psalm 73: 28: "But as for me, it is good to be near God. I have made the Sovereign Lord my refuge; I will tell of all your deeds."

6

Psalm 140: 7: "O Sovereign Lord, my strong deliverer, who shields my head in the day of battle."

7

Psalm 107: 14: "He brought them out of darkness and the deepest gloom and broke away their chains."

MAY

After Action Report (AAR)

1

Countdown
DAY

2

Countdown
DAY

3

Countdown
DAY

4

Countdown
DAY

5

Countdown
DAY

6

Countdown
DAY

7

Countdown
DAY

MAY

Bible Update Brief

8

VE DAY

Psalm 102: 2: "Do not hide your face from me when I am in distress. Turn your ear to me when I call, answer me quickly."

9

Psalm 60: 12: "With God we will gain the victory, and He will trample down our enemies."

10

Psalm 31: 24: "Be strong and take heart, all you who hope in the Lord."

11

Psalm 38: 22: "Come quickly to help me, O Lord my Savior."

12

Psalm 44: 6-7: "I do not trust in my bow, my sword does not give me victory; but you give us victory over our enemies, you put our adversaries to shame."

13

Psalm 145: 20: "The Lord watches over all who love Him, but all the wicked He will destroy."

14

Psalm 103: 17: "But from everlasting to everlasting the Lord's love is with them who fear Him, and His righteousness with their children's children."

MAY

After Action Report (AAR)

8

Countdown
DAY

9

Countdown
DAY

10

Countdown
DAY

11

Countdown
DAY

12

Countdown
DAY

13

Countdown
DAY

14

Countdown
DAY

MAY

Bible Update Brief

15

Psalm 36: 10: "Continue your love to those who know you, your righteousness to the upright in heart."

16

Psalm 31: 18: "Let their lying lips be silenced for with pride and contempt they speak arrogantly against the righteous."

17

Psalm 67: 1: "May God be gracious to us and bless us and make His face to shine upon us."

18

Psalm 85: 8a: "I will listen to what God, the Lord will say; He promises peace to His people, His saints."

19

Psalm 107: 13: "Then they cried to the Lord in their trouble, and He saved them from their distress."

20

Psalm 37: 4: "Delight yourself in the Lord and He will give you the desires of your heart."

21

Psalm 31: 22: "In my alarm I said, 'I am cut off from your sight!' Yet you heard my cry for mercy when I called to you for help."

MAY

After Action Report (AAR)

15

Countdown
DAY

16

Countdown
DAY

17

Countdown
DAY

18

Countdown
DAY

19

Countdown
DAY

20

Countdown
DAY

21

Countdown
DAY

MAY

22

Psalm 121: 8: "The Lord will watch over your coming and going both now and forevermore."

23

Psalm 64: 2: "Hide me from the conspiracy of the wicked, from that noisy crowd of evildoers."

24

Psalm 68: 1: "May God arise, may His enemies be scattered, may His foes flee before Him."

25

Psalm 112: 1: "Blessed is the man who fears the Lord, who finds great delight in His commands."

26

Psalm 57: 2: "I cry out to God Most High, to God, who fulfills His purposes for me."

27

Psalm 23: 3: "He restores my soul. He guides me in paths of righteousness for His name's sake."

28

Psalm 73: 23: "Yet I am always with you; you hold me by my right hand."

MAY

After Action Report (AAR)

22

Countdown
DAY

23

Countdown
DAY

24

Countdown
DAY

25

Countdown
DAY

26

Countdown
DAY

27

Countdown
DAY

28

Countdown
DAY

MAY

Bible Update Brief

29

Psalm 86: 2: "Guard my life, for I am devoted to you. You are my God; save your servant who trusts in you."

30

MEMORIAL DAY

Psalm 105: 5: "Remember the wonders He has done, His miracles, and the judgments He pronounced."

31

Psalm 139: 8: "If I go up the heavens, you are there; if I make my bed in the depths you are there."

MAY

After Action Report (AAR)

29

Countdown
DAY

30

Countdown
DAY

31

Countdown
DAY

NOTES

Psalm 42:1
"As the deer pants for streams of water,
so my soul pants for you, O God."

WORDS OF ENCOURAGEMENT

(from an e-mail to my son from June 6, 2004)

Good morning Soldier-Son,

Today is a special day in several respects. It is the sixtieth anniversary of D-Day; it is the day after former President Reagan, one of the greatest patriot presidents we have been honored to have and who put our military back together and bolstered the American spirit, has passed away. It is also a day for me to tell you, my son, what I think of your courage, the duty you are performing at great risk, and your sacrifice of a piece of your life for a great cause.

I know Garry and I tell you every time we write how proud we are of you. Don't take these words lightly, because they are not meant lightly. Sometimes you think less of yourself than you ought to think…that you are where you are because of things you did not do. Son, you are there because of who and what you are inside. You are a brave, patriotic, strong, and courageous man with conviction and purpose. You are a born leader, one who sees a difficult situation and does not think why something can't be done but HOW it can be accomplished. You have humor that helps to ease the overly distraught emotions that come in wartime. You are a warrior…a Christian warrior who is ruled by a strength and resolve greater than your own. What you are being asked to do is most difficult, but you understand in your heart and mind that your namesake (David) was a warrior like you. He had to do difficult things and still maintain his heart…he did through his relationship with Almighty God.

Today, I watched President Bush's speech at Normandy honoring survivors as well as all those young men who died on those beaches sixty years ago. He spoke of their courage and faith…I remembered them by thinking of you with tears of pride, joy, and great love. Thank you, my dear son, for answering the call of this hour for your country. I could never be more proud of you or wish any greater honor than what you are accomplishing on that hot, foreign soil, so far from home and all that you love…what a fine soldier and son!

JUNE

Bible Update Brief

1

Psalm 27: 3: "Though an army besiege me, my heart will not fear; though war break out against me, even then will I be confident."

2

Psalm 119: 40: "How I long for your precepts! Preserve my life in your righteousness."

3

Psalm 91: 9-10: "If you make the Most High your dwelling-even the Lord, who is my refuge-then no harm will befall you, no disaster will come near your tent."

4

Psalm 139: 3-4: "You discern my going out and my lying down; you are familiar with all my ways. Before a word is on my tongue, you know it completely, O Lord."

5

Psalm 102: 1: "Hear my prayer, O Lord; let my cry for help come to you."

6

D-DAY

Psalm 62: 8: "Trust in Him at all times, O people; pour out your hearts to Him, for God is our refuge."

7

Psalm 55: 16: "But I call to God, and the Lord saves me."

JUNE

After Action Report (AAR)

1

DAY

2

Countdown
DAY

3

Countdown
DAY

4

Countdown
DAY

5

Countdown
DAY

6

Countdown
DAY

7

Countdown
DAY

JUNE

Bible Update Brief

8

Psalm 139: 5: "You hem me in-behind and before; you have laid your hand upon me."

9

Psalm 62: 11: "One thing God has spoken, two things have I heard; that you, O God, are strong, and that you, O Lord are loving."

10

Psalm 89: 2: "I will declare that your love stands firm forever, that you established your faithfulness in heaven itself."

11

Psalm 66: 20: "Praise be to God, who has not rejected my prayer or withheld His love from me."

12

Psalm 31: 20a: "In the shelter of your presence you hide them from the intrigues of men."

13

Psalm 112: 4: "Even in darkness light dawns for the upright, for the gracious and compassionate and righteous man."

14

Psalm 92: 11: "My eyes have seen the defeat of my adversaries; my ears have heard the rout of my wicked foes."

JUNE

After Action Report (AAR)

8

Countdown
DAY

9

Countdown
DAY

10

Countdown
DAY

11

Countdown
DAY

12

Countdown
DAY

13

Countdown
DAY

14

Countdown
DAY

JUNE

Bible Update Brief

15

Psalm 111: 10: "The fear of the Lord is the beginning of wisdom; all who follow His precepts have good understanding. To Him belongs eternal praise."

16

Psalm 144: 15: "Blessed are the people of whom this is true; blessed are the people whose God is the Lord."

17

Psalm 86: 13: "For great is your love toward me; you have delivered me from the depths of the grave."

18

Psalm 125: 2: "As the mountains surround Jerusalem, so the Lord surrounds His people both now and forevermore."

19

Psalm 44: 5: "Through you we push back our enemies; through your name we trample our foes."

20

Psalm 89: 15: "Blessed are those who have learned to acclaim you, who walk in the light of your presence, O Lord."

21

Psalm 118: 13: "I was pushed back and about to fall, but the Lord helped me."

JUNE

After Action Report (AAR)

15

Countdown
DAY

16

Countdown
DAY

17

Countdown
DAY

18

Countdown
DAY

19

Countdown
DAY

20

Countdown
DAY

21

Countdown
DAY

JUNE

Bible Update Brief

22

Psalm 23: 4: "Even though I walk through the valley of the shadow of death, I will fear no evil, for you are with me; your rod and staff, they comfort me."

23

Psalm 119: 66: "Teach me knowledge and good judgement, for I believe in your commands."

24

Psalm 27: 5b-6a: "He will hide me in the shelter of His tabernacle and set me high on a rock. Then my head will be exalted above the enemies who surround me..."

25

Psalm 103: 13: "As a father has compassion of his children, so the Lord has compassion on those who fear Him."

26

Psalm 112: 3: "Surely, he will never be shaken; a righteous man will be remembered forever."

27

Psalm 103: 12: "As far as the east is from the west, so far has He removed our transgressions from us."

28

Psalm 5: 12: "For surely O Lord, you bless the righteous; you surround them with your favor as with a shield."

JUNE

After Action Report (AAR)

22

Countdown
DAY

23

Countdown
DAY

24

Countdown
DAY

25

Countdown
DAY

26

Countdown
DAY

27

Countdown
DAY

28

Countdown
DAY

JUNE

Bible Update Brief

29

Psalm 118: 5: "In my anguish, I cried to the Lord, and He answered by setting me free."

30

Psalm 25: 21: "May integrity and uprightness protect me, because my hope is in you."

JUNE

After Action Report (AAR)

29

Countdown
DAY

30

Countdown
DAY

NOTES

NOTES

NOTES

WORDS OF ENCOURAGEMENT

(from an e-mail to my son, July 9, 2004)

Hi Son,

I feel the need to pray over your spirit. Please take the burden of your war experiences, put them in a wheelbarrow, and roll them up to Jesus. That is the picture I have in my mind when releasing unbearable hurts in my life. I know I cannot imagine what you have endured and that you must wonder if you can ever let go of the anxiety in your mind of what you have seen. I have not had visible images to deal with, but I have had terrible imprints of unfathomable hurts that I had to let rise up to my conscious so I could take them in my wheelbarrow to the cross....

Our fathers, your grandfathers, had to perform duties, see unmentionable sights of war, yet they came home. In time, many dealt with the TV monitors inside their minds and had to release them. They went on to be wonderful husbands, fathers, and, as you know, grandfathers. It doesn't mean they "forgot" everything, but they were led by God to give it to Him.

When we have been touched by the kind of evil we cannot even decipher, it leaves us almost blank emotionally...but only periodically, if we know where to "dump it." I pray this does not come across as any kind of lecture, Sweetheart. I know by the Holy Spirit's impression to me that you are going through some internal suffering.

God will make a way for you to process your war experience. I understand that He will use someone who can readily identify with what you have gone through. I promise this will happen. You have been asked to be a warrior...there is great honor when the cause is for freedom from oppression for others. When you get a chance, look up what David went through in warfare. You will find his story in 1 Samuel, 2 Samuel, and 1 Kings and 2 Kings. Most of his days he spent in great combat. His special warriors are listed with honor. You will read some of the horrors they went through. Psalm 23 talks about the valley of the shadow of death...of spreading a banquet in the presence of his enemies. These words were written in some of his darkest days....

"Even though I walk through the valley of the shadow of death, I will fear no evil, for you are with me; your rod and your staff, they comfort me...."

JULY

Bible Update Brief

1

Psalm 138: 8a: "The Lord will fulfill His purpose for me…"

2

Psalm 86: 14: "Bring joy to your servant, for to you, O Lord, I lift up my soul."

3

Psalm 71: 2: "Rescue and deliver me in your righteousness; turn your ear to me and save me."

4

INDEPENDANCE
DAY

Psalm 118: 6: "The Lord is with me; I will not be afraid. What can man do to me?"

5

Psalm 106: 1: "Praise the Lord. Give thanks to the Lord, for He is good; His love endures forever."

6

Psalm 84: 2: "My soul yearns, even faints, for the courts of the Lord; my heart and my flesh cry out for the living God."

7

Psalm 103: 14: "For He knows how we are formed, he remembers that we are dust."

JULY

After Action Report (AAR)

1

Countdown
DAY

2

Countdown
DAY

3

Countdown
DAY

4

Countdown
DAY

5

Countdown
DAY

6

Countdown
DAY

7

Countdown
DAY

JULY

Bible Update Brief

8

Psalm 85: 6: "Will you not revive us again, that your people may rejoice in you?"

9

Psalm 94: 12-13: "Blessed is the man you discipline, O Lord, the man you teach from your law; you grant Him relief from days of trouble, till a pit is dug for the wicked."

10

Psalm 33: 15, 18: "No king is saved by the size of the army; no warrior escapes by His great strength...But the eyes of the Lord are on those who fear Him, on those whose hope is in His unfailing love."

11

Psalm 29: 11: "The Lord gives strength to His people; the Lord blesses His people with peace."

12

Psalm 62: 2: "He alone is my rock and my salvation; He is my fortress, I will never be shaken."

13

Psalm 3: 8: "From the Lord comes deliverance. May your blessing be on your people."

14

Psalm 3: 4-5: "To the Lord I cry aloud and he answers me from His holy hill. I lie down and sleep; I wake again because the Lord sustains me."

JULY

After Action Report (AAR)

8

Countdown
DAY

9

Countdown
DAY

10

Countdown
DAY

11

Countdown
DAY

12

Countdown
DAY

13

Countdown
DAY

14

Countdown
DAY

JULY

Bible Update Brief

15

Psalm 149: 6: "May the praise of God be in their mouths and a double-edged sword in their hand."

16

Psalm 119: 114: "You are my refuge and my shield; I have put my hope in your word."

17

Psalm 37: 9: "For evil men will be cut off, but those who hope in the Lord will inherit the land."

18

Psalm 102: 17: "He will respond to the prayer of the destitute; He will not despise their plea."

19

Psalm 34: 7: "The angel of the Lord encamps around those who fear Him, and He delivers them."

20

Psalm 46: 2: "Therefore we will not fear, though the earth give way and the mountains fall into the heart of the sea."

21

Psalm 95: 4: "In His hands are the depth of the earth, and the mountain peaks belong to Him."

JULY

After Action Report (AAR)

15

Countdown
DAY

16

Countdown
DAY

17

Countdown
DAY

18

Countdown
DAY

19

Countdown
DAY

20

Countdown
DAY

21

Countdown
DAY

JULY

Bible Update Brief

22

Psalm 85: 11: "Faithfulness springs forth from the earth, and righteousness looks down from heaven."

23

Psalm 31: 3: "Since you are my rock and my fortress, for the sake of your name lead and guide me."

24

Psalm 116: 2: "Because he turned His ear to me, I will call on Him as long as I live."

25

Psalm 60: 5: "Save us and help us with your right hand that those you love may be delivered."

26

Psalm 91: 15: "He will call upon me, and I will answer Him; I will be with Him in trouble, I will deliver Him and honor Him."

27

Psalm 34: 18: "The Lord is close to the brokenhearted and saves those who are crushed in spirit."

28

Psalm 45: 3: "Gird your sword upon your side, O mighty one; clothe yourself with splendor and majesty."

JULY

After Action Report (AAR)

22

Countdown
DAY

23

Countdown
DAY

24

Countdown
DAY

25

Countdown
DAY

26

Countdown
DAY

27

Countdown
DAY

28

Countdown
DAY

JULY
Bible Update Brief

29

Psalm 118: 7: "The Lord is with me; He is my helper. I will look in triumph on my enemies."

30

Psalm 34: 17: "The righteous cry out, and the Lord hears them; He delivers them from all their troubles."

JULY

After Action Report (AAR)

29

Countdown
DAY

30

Countdown
DAY

NOTES

NOTES

NOTES

WORDS OF ENCOURAGEMENT

(excerpt from an e-mail from August 12, 2004)

Dearest Son,

Today I know you have been through the greatest stresses of intenseness. You and your fellow soldiers are on my heart and in my prayers. I have been following the news throughout the day. I know there are more days to come.

May the Lord strengthen you and preserve and protect all that concerns you in your mission right now. I love you very, very much.

May courage from God rise up to meet you at every turn, in tight, dark places, and may His mighty warring angels go ahead of you and expose any danger ahead of time.

May God's mighty right arm sustain you and may Jesus encourage your heart and keep your mind focused, your eyesight sharp, and your aim exact and expediently dispersed.

May you know in your "knower" that He is with you every step you take. May you all be kept safe in the battle's fiercest moments. May the enemy of life and life's precious freedoms be dealt the deadliest of defeats.

May your slight moments of rest be as though they were full nights of sleep. May the supernatural power of God keep you from the devastation of fear.

This is my prayer, this is my heart with all my love,

Mom

AUGUST

Bible Update Brief

1

Psalm 59: 1: "Deliver me from my enemies, O God; protect me from those who rise up against me."

2

Psalm 60: 4: "But for those who fear you, you have raised a banner to be unfurled against the bow."

3

Psalm 116: 1: "I love the Lord, for He heard my voice; He heard my cry for mercy."

4

Psalm 68: 19: "Praise be to the Lord, to God our Savior, who daily bears our burdens."

5

Psalm 56: 4: "In God, whose word I praise, in God I trust; I will not be afraid. What can mortal man do to me?"

6

Psalm 89: 17: "For you are their glory and strength, and by your favor you exalt our horn."

7

Psalm 91: 2: "I will say of the Lord, He is my refuge and my fortress, my God, in whom I trust."

AUGUST

After Action Report (AAR)

1

Countdown
DAY

2

Countdown
DAY

3

Countdown
DAY

4

Countdown
DAY

5

Countdown
DAY

6

Countdown
DAY

7

Countdown
DAY

AUGUST

Bible Update Brief

8

Psalm 89: 14: "Righteousness and justice are the foundation of your throne; love and faithfulness go before you."

9

Psalm 56: 3: "When I am afraid, I will trust in you."

10

Psalm 27: 5a: "For in the day of trouble, He will keep me safe in His dwelling."

11

Psalm 86: 6: "Hear my prayer, O Lord, Listen to my cry for mercy."

12

Psalm 91: 7: "A thousand may fall at your side, ten thousand at your right hand, but it will not come near you."

13

Psalm 55: 9a: "Confuse the wicked, O Lord, confound their speech."

14

Psalm 103: 10: "He does not treat us as our sins deserve or repay us according to our iniquities."

AUGUST

After Action Report (AAR)

8

Countdown
DAY

9

Countdown
DAY

10

Countdown
DAY

11

Countdown
DAY

12

Countdown
DAY

13

Countdown
DAY

14

Countdown
DAY

AUGUST

Bible Update Brief

15

Psalm 89: 1: "I will sing of the Lord's great love forever; with my mouth I will make your faithfulness known through all generations."

16

Psalm 103: 1: "Praise the Lord, O my soul; all my inmost being, praise His holy name."

17

Psalm 86: 7: "In the day of my trouble, I will call to you, for you will answer me."

18

Psalm 23: 6: "Surely goodness and love will follow me all the days of my life, and I will dwell in the house of the Lord forever."

19

Psalm 69: 16: "Answer me, O Lord, out of the goodness of your love; in your great mercy turn to me."

20

Psalm 91: 3: "Surely He will save you from the fowler's snare and from the deadly pestilence."

21

Psalm 36: 11-12: "May the foot of the proud not come against me, nor the hand of the wicked drive me away. See how the evildoers lie fallen-thrown down, not able to rise!"

AUGUST

After Action Report (AAR)

15

Countdown
DAY

16

Countdown
DAY

17

Countdown
DAY

18

Countdown
DAY

19

Countdown
DAY

20

Countdown
DAY

21

Countdown
DAY

AUGUST

Bible Update Brief

22

Psalm 34: 1: "I will extol the Lord at all times; His praise will always be on my lips."

23

Psalm 73: 26: "My flesh and my heart may fail, but God is the strength of my heart and my portion forever."

24

Psalm 103: 5: "Who satisfies your desires with good things so that your strength is renewed like the eagles."

25

Psalm 4: 1: "Answer me when I call to you, O my righteous God. Give me relief from my distress; be merciful to me and hear my prayer."

26

Psalm 119: 35: "Direct me in the path of your commands, for there I find delight."

27

Psalm 91: 11: "For He will command His angels concerning you to guard you in all your ways."

28

Psalm 108: 13: "With God we will gain the victory, and He will trample down our enemies."

AUGUST

After Action Report (AAR)

22

Countdown
DAY

23

Countdown
DAY

24

Countdown
DAY

25

Countdown
DAY

26

Countdown
DAY

27

Countdown
DAY

28

Countdown
DAY

AUGUST

Bible Update Brief

29

Psalm 86: 11: "Teach me your way, O Lord, and I will walk in your truth; give me an undivided heart that I may fear your name."

30

Psalm 63: 8: "My soul clings to you; your right hand upholds me."

31

Psalm 31: 21: "Praise be to the Lord, for He showed His wonderful love to me when I was in a besieged city."

AUGUST

After Action Report (AAR)

29

Countdown
DAY

30

Countdown
DAY

31

Countdown
DAY

NOTES

Psalm 91:4: A
"He will cover you with his feathers, and under
His wings you will find refuge."

WORDS OF ENCOURAGEMENT

(from an excerpt of an e-mail from July 9, 2004)

Son,

We all question our normalcy when we have gone through terrible things. I cannot tell you how many times I have wondered in my life if I were really going to be all right after some of my great battles. I still face those and must get out my wheelbarrow and load it up, roll it over to Jesus, and let him put it into the cross. I tell Him exactly how I feel…usually very unspiritual, sometimes full of anger, sometimes so sad that all I can do is cry until I can hardly breathe. Sometimes I feel so dead emotionally that there are no emotions. That is a scary place to me. But God is always faithful to meet me right where I am.

I have dealt with a lot of fear and depression in my life, Son. That may sound funny to you, but that is where my faith always begins, grows, and prospers…when I know that I have absolutely nothing but gut-wrenching fear to bring to Him and ask for His comfort and help. He gives it, and I rise up above my paralyzing fear and begin again in renewed faith.

And did I mention tiredness? That one really gets me because when I am particularly fatigued, I can't make sense of anything. Stress seems out of control at those moments and I even question my own mind.

Son, I don't know if any of this helps but it is my own journey, day in, day out, one day at a time. I hope this honesty of heart of my own struggles doesn't discourage what you thought of your mother's faith…it is not my faith that is something to speak of nearly so much as it is HIS GREATNESS to keep us, help us, and deliver us through impossible passages and places.

I love you so very much. My heart hurts when yours does. But I know the One who made you will keep you and deliver you, WHOLE and COMPLETE. Take care, my beloved son.

SEPTEMBER

Bible Update Brief

1

Psalm 91: 1: "He who dwells in the shelter of the Most High will rest in the shadow of the Almighty."

2

VJ DAY

Psalm 64: 10: "Let the righteous rejoice in the Lord and take refuge in Him; let all the upright in heart praise Him."

3

Psalm 71: 20a: "Though you have made me see troubles, many and bitter, you will restore my life again..."

4

Psalm 51: 10: "Create in me a pure heart, O God, and renew a steadfast spirit within me."

5

Psalm 94: 9: "Does not He who implanted the ear not hear? Does He who formed the eye not see?"

6

Psalm 121: 3: "He will not let your foot slip-He who watches over you will not slumber."

7

Psalm 108: 12: "Give us aid against the enemy, for the help of man is worthless."

SEPTEMBER

After Action Report (AAR)

1

Countdown
DAY

2

Countdown
DAY

3

Countdown
DAY

4

Countdown
DAY

5

Countdown
DAY

6

Countdown
DAY

7

Countdown
DAY

SEPTEMBER

Bible Update Brief

8

Psalm 63: 3: "Because your love is better than life, my lips will glorify you."

9

Psalm 33: 4: "For the word of the Lord is right and true: He is faithful in all He does."

10

Psalm 59: 16: "But I will sing of your strength in the morning, I will sing of your love; for you are my fortress, my refuge in times of trouble."

11

Psalm 90: 12: "Teach us to number our days aright, that we may gain a heart of wisdom."

12

Psalm 4: 8: "I will lie down and sleep in peace, for you alone, O Lord, make me dwell in safety."

13

Psalm 116: 8-9: "For you, O Lord, have delivered my soul from death, my eyes from tears, my feet from stumbling, that I may walk before the Lord in the land of the living."

14

Psalm 59: 2: "Deliver me from evildoers, and save me from bloodthirsty men."

SEPTEMBER

After Action Report (AAR)

8 _____

_____

_____

| Countdown |
| DAY |

9 _____

_____

_____

| Countdown |
| DAY |

10 _____

_____

_____

| Countdown |
| DAY |

11 _____

_____

_____

| Countdown |
| DAY |

12 _____

_____

_____

| Countdown |
| DAY |

13 _____

_____

_____

| Countdown |
| DAY |

14 _____

_____

_____

| Countdown |
| DAY |

SEPTEMBER

Bible Update Brief

15

Psalm 62: 1: "My soul finds rest in God alone; my salvation comes from Him."

16

Psalm 124: 8: "Our help is in the name of the Lord, the Maker of heaven and earth."

17

Psalm 68: 28: "Summon your power, O God; show us your strength, O God, as you have done before."

18

Psalm 57: 10: "For great is your love, reaching to the heavens; your faithfulness reaches to the skies."

19

Psalm 69: 18: "Come near and rescue me; redeem me because of my foes."

20

Psalm 115: 15: "May you be blessed by the Lord, the Maker of heaven and earth."

21

Psalm 20: 1: "May the Lord answer you when you are in distress; may the name of God of Jacob protect you."

SEPTEMBER

After Action Report (AAR)

15

Countdown
DAY

16

Countdown
DAY

17

Countdown
DAY

18

Countdown
DAY

19

Countdown
DAY

20

Countdown
DAY

21

Countdown
DAY

SEPTEMBER

Bible Update Brief

22

Psalm 63: 1: "O God, you are my God, earnestly I seek you; my soul thirsts for you, my body longs for you, in a dry and weary land where there is no water."

23

Psalm 89: 16: "They rejoice in your name all day long; they exult in your righteousness."

24

Psalm 86: 1: "Hear, O Lord, and answer me, for I am poor and needy."

25

Psalm 46: 1: "God is our refuge and strength, an ever present help in time of trouble."

26

Psalm 100: 3: "Know that the Lord is God. It is He who made us, and we are His, we are His people, the sheep of His pasture."

27

Psalm 36: 7: "How priceless is your unfailing love! Both high and low among men find refuge in the shadow of your wings."

28

Psalm 91: 4: "He will cover you with His feathers, and under His wings you will find refuge, His faithfulness will be your shield..."

SEPTEMBER

After Action Report (AAR)

22

Countdown
DAY

23

Countdown
DAY

24

Countdown
DAY

25

Countdown
DAY

26

Countdown
DAY

27

Countdown
DAY

28

Countdown
DAY

SEPTEMBER

Bible Update Brief

29

Psalm 85: 10: "Love and faithfulness meet together; righteousness and peace kiss each other."

30

Psalm 37: 14-15: "The wicked draw the sword and bend the bow to bring down the poor and needy, to slay those whose ways are upright. But their sword will pierce their own hearts, and their bows will be broken."

SEPTEMBER

After Action Report (AAR)

29

Countdown
DAY

30

Countdown
DAY

NOTES

NOTES

NOTES

WORDS OF ENCOURAGEMENT

(excerpt of an e-mail from October 4, 2004)

Top of the mornin', Sarge,

I pray that you are well today…May you rejoice in God…
The One and Only God
Divine Commander-in-chief…
Savior, Creator, Inspirer, Healer, and Deliverer
The One Who Sees the earth from eternity;
The Conqueror of all evil,
The Master Architect of the universe,
The One who is beyond all time, space, and dimension,
Encourager of our hearts, Living God,
Supreme Lover of the souls of men everywhere,
Forgiveness Personified,
The All in All, Truth, Light, Peace, and Strength, and High Tower
Shepherd of our lives,
Lifter of our heads,
The Gate to heaven…
The Intercessor of our hearts…Originator of prayer,
Friend of all friends,
The Keeper of our minds, hearts, and souls,
The Father who never fails,
The Patient, Gracious God,
The One who never leaves us nor forsakes us,
The Restorer of broken hearts and broken lives…
The Rewarder and the Gift Giver,
Supernatural and Supreme Power,
The Ever-Alert One who never slumbers nor sleeps…
Miracle Maker and Renewer of faith
The One who knows the number of hairs on our heads…
The Increaser of true good…

Be blessed in Him…all day, every day, in good and bad times—and in battle, may He be your Fear-Taker and your Peace-Giver!

OCTOBER

Bible Update Brief

1

Psalm 103: 4: "Who redeems your life from the pit and crowns you with love and compassion."

2

Psalm 23: 2: "He makes me lie down in green pastures, He leads me beside still waters."

3

Psalm 86: 3: "Have mercy on me, O Lord, for I call to you all day long."

4

Psalm 86: 5: "You are forgiving and good, O Lord, abounding in love to all who call to you."

5

Psalm 59: 9: "O my strength, I watch for you; you, O God, are my fortress, my loving God."

6

Psalm 36: 6: "Your righteousness is like the mighty mountains, your justice like the great deep."

7

Psalm 28: 7: "The Lord is my strength and my shield; my heart trusts in Him, and I am helped."

OCTOBER

After Action Report (AAR)

1

Countdown
DAY

2

Countdown
DAY

3

Countdown
DAY

4

Countdown
DAY

5

Countdown
DAY

6

Countdown
DAY

7

Countdown
DAY

OCTOBER

Bible Update Brief

8

Psalm 31: 4: "Free me from the trap that is set for me, for you are my refuge."

9

Psalm 93: 4: "Mightier than the thunder of great waters, mightier than the breakers of the sea-the Lord on high is mighty."

10

Psalm 145: 14: "The Lord upholds all those who fall and lifts up all who are bowed down."

11

Psalm 43: 3a: "Send forth your light and your truth, let them guide me."

12

COLUMBUS DAY

Psalm 66: 9: "He has preserved our lives and kept our feet from slipping."

13

Psalm 71: 4: "Deliver me, O my God, from the hand of the wicked, from the grasp of evil and cruel men."

14

Psalm 69: 17: "Do not hide your face from your servant; answer me quickly, for I am in trouble."

OCTOBER

After Action Report (AAR)

8

Countdown
DAY

9

Countdown
DAY

10

Countdown
DAY

11

Countdown
DAY

12

Countdown
DAY

13

Countdown
DAY

14

Countdown
DAY

OCTOBER

Bible Update Brief

15

Psalm 84: 11: "For the Lord God is a sun and shield; the Lord bestows favor and honor; no good thing does He withhold from those whose walk is blameless."

16

Psalm 142: 3: "When my spirit grows faint within me, it is you who know my way."

17

Psalm 72: 4: "He will defend the afflicted among the people and save the children of the needy; he will crush the oppressor."

18

Psalm 121: 1-2: "I lift up my eyes to the hills-where does my help come from? My help comes from the Lord, the Maker of heaven and earth."

19

Psalm 119: 50: "My comfort in my suffering is this; your promise preserves my life."

20

Psalm 97: 11: "Light is shed upon the righteous and joy on the upright in heart."

21

Psalm 32: 10: "Many are the woes of the wicked, but the Lord's unfailing love surrounds the man who trusts in Him."

OCTOBER

After Action Report (AAR)

15

Countdown
DAY

16

Countdown
DAY

17

Countdown
DAY

18

Countdown
DAY

19

Countdown
DAY

20

Countdown
DAY

21

Countdown
DAY

OCTOBER

Bible Update Brief

22

Psalm 31: 19a: "How great is your goodness, which you have stored up for those who fear you, which you bestow in the sight of men on those who take refuge in you."

23

Psalm 31: 15: "My times are in your hands; deliver me from my enemies and from those who pursue me."

24

Psalm 61: 2: "From the ends of the earth I call to you, I call as my heart grows faint; lead me to the rock that is higher than I."

25

Psalm 68: 17a: "The chariots of God are tens of thousands and thousands of thousands."

26

Psalm 121: 5-6: "The Lord watches over you-the Lord is your shade at your right hand; the sun will not harm you by day, nor the moon by night."

27

Psalm 145: 18: "The Lord is near to all who call on Him, to all who call on Him in truth."

28

Psalm 64: 1: "Hear me, O God, as I voice my complaint; protect my life from the threat of the enemy."

OCTOBER

After Action Report (AAR)

22

Countdown
DAY

23

Countdown
DAY

24

Countdown
DAY

25

Countdown
DAY

26

Countdown
DAY

27

Countdown
DAY

28

Countdown
DAY

OCTOBER

Bible Update Brief

29

Psalm 18: 2: "The Lord is my rock, my fortress and my deliver; my God is my rock, in whom I take refuge. He is my shield and the horn of my salvation, my stronghold."

30

Psalm 34: 19: "A righteous man may have many troubles; but the Lord delivers him from them all."

31

HALLOWEEN

Psalm 28: 8: "The Lord is the strength of His people, a fortress of salvation for His anointed one."

OCTOBER

After Action Report (AAR)

29

30

31

NOTES

Psalm 23: 1-2
"The Lord is my shepherd, I shall not be in want. He makes me lie down in green pictures, He leads me beside quiet waters."

WORDS OF ENCOURAGEMENT

(from an e-mail to my son, December 16, 2004)

Good morning Son,

It is a new day with hope in my heart and I pray in yours as well. I do not know what I would do without my hope in Jesus. You know, it isn't just a word, and it isn't about tomorrow but about today. So many times just this week, He has given me literal signs of hope. I had some discouragement, but He brought me through it and out of it by the simplicity of my hope in Him. He used others' kind messages, e-mails, and phone calls. Something rises out of nowhere (actually, the Great Somewhere), fills your heart, and restores your pathway with clarity of purpose, leaving the unanswered questions in more capable hands than mine. He lifts your spirit to soar above heartache, loneliness, sadness, and trouble. What a God we serve! What an intercessor we have in Jesus!

I continue to pray for your panic attacks. I just read a lengthy article on a report about what our soldiers in Iraq and Afghanistan are going through concerning this. I truly believe there will be a turnaround and that more help will be available for the problems brought on by what all of you have experienced and seen....

When I was in the 10th grade, I saw pictures of the holocaust…just pictures, but they so profoundly affected me as to the horrors of what evil will do to men, women, and children, that I devoted a section to it in my history classes later on when I became a teacher. I had trouble with those pictures and asked to be a force for good in this world against such evil. I never dreamed I would one day have a son who would literally fight the kind of evil I saw in those pictures so many years ago.

Dearest Son, thank you for daring to be part of such an unbelievable undertaking that has been so costly on your heart and mind as well as your body. Thank you for taking courage; for trusting God; for bearing the great pain of war; for eliminating evil…I wish you could peek into my heart and feel what it feels for you. I wish I could wrap my arms around and comfort you like when you were just a boy. A mother could not be more proud of her son than I am.

I pray the peace that passes understanding will surround your heart and mind. I pray the strength of angelic forces around you; I pray the hope of Jesus to fill you up; I pray the love of God to lift you up. We will be here for you and we will listen when you need to talk. Our shoulders are here for you to let out any emotions you need to. We are not weak and don't need protection against anything you need to unload, for we are soldiers, too, made strong by compassions formed in adversity.... Do not let these things go down into a cavernous abyss of suppressed darkness. Only what is brought to the light can heal.

Take heart, let the Lifter of your head point you on to finish your tasks with His strength.

NOVEMBER

Bible Update Brief

1

Psalm 80: 3: "Restore us, O God; make your face shine upon us, that we may be saved."

2

Psalm 100: 4: "Enter His gates with thanksgiving and His courts with praise; give thanks to Him and praise His name."

3

Psalm 7: 10: "My shield is God most High, who saves the upright in heart."

4

Psalm 34: 22: "The Lord redeems His servants; no one will be condemned who takes refuge in Him."

5

Psalm 104: 2: "He wraps Himself in light as with a garment; he stretches out the heavens as a tent."

6

Psalm 91: 11-12: "For He will command His angels concerning you to guard you in all your ways; they will lift you up in their hands, so that you will not strike your foot against a stone."

7

Psalm 37: 17: "For the power of the wicked will be broken, but the Lord upholds the righteous."

NOVEMBER

After Action Report (AAR)

1

Countdown
DAY

2

Countdown
DAY

3

Countdown
DAY

4

Countdown
DAY

5

Countdown
DAY

6

Countdown
DAY

7

Countdown
DAY

NOVEMBER

Bible Update Brief

8

Psalm 25: 1-2: "To you, O Lord, I lift up my soul; in you I trust, O my God. Do not let me be put to shame, nor let my enemies triumph over me."

9

Psalm 84: 5a: "Blessed are those whose strength is in you."

10

Psalm 33: 22: "May your unfailing love rest upon us, O Lord, even as we put our hope in you."

11

VETERAN'S DAY

Psalm 139: 16b: "...All the days ordained for me were written in your book before one of them came to be."

12

Psalm 34: 8: "Taste and see that the Lord is good; blessed is the man who takes refuge in Him."

13

Psalm 38: 9-10: "All my longings lie open before you, O Lord; my sighing is not hidden from you. My heart pounds, my strength fails me; even the light has gone from my eyes."

14

Psalm 30: 2: "O Lord my God, I called to you for help and you healed me."

NOVEMBER

After Action Report (AAR)

8

Countdown
DAY

9

Countdown
DAY

10

Countdown
DAY

11

Countdown
DAY

12

Countdown
DAY

13

Countdown
DAY

14

Countdown
DAY

NOVEMBER

Bible Update Brief

15

Psalm 71: 1: "In you, O Lord, I have taken refuge; let me never be put to shame."

16

Psalm 139: 7: "Where can I go from your Spirit? Where can I flee from your presence.?"

17

Psalm 33: 5: "The Lord loves righteousness and justice; the earth is full of His unfailing love."

18

Psalm 116: 3-4: "The cords of death entangled me, the anguish of the grave came upon me; I was overcome by trouble and sorrow. Then I called on the name of the Lord: 'O Lord, save me!'"

19

Psalm 116: 7: "Be at rest once more, O my soul, for the Lord has been good to you."

20

Psalm 18: 3: "I call to the Lord, who is worthy of praise, and I am saved from my enemies."

21

Psalm 99: 3-4a: "Let them praise your great and awesome name-He is holy. The King is mighty, He loves justice-you have established equity."

NOVEMBER

After Action Report (AAR)

15

Countdown
DAY

16

Countdown
DAY

17

Countdown
DAY

18

Countdown
DAY

19

Countdown
DAY

20

Countdown
DAY

21

Countdown
DAY

NOVEMBER

Bible Update Brief

22

Psalm 66: 5: "Come and see what God has done, how awesome His works in man's behalf!"

23

Psalm 91: 14: "Because he loves me, says the Lord, "I will rescue him; I will protect him for He acknowledges my name."

24

Psalm 20: 8: "They are brought to their knees and fall, but we rise up and stand firm."

25

THANKSGIVING

Psalm 94: 22: "But the Lord has become my fortress, and my God the rock in whom I take refuge."

26

Psalm 31: 16: "Let your face shine on your servant; save me in your unfailing love."

27

Psalm 101: 1: "I will sing of your love and justice; to you, O Lord, I will sing praise."

28

Psalm 17: 7: "Show the wonder of your great love, you who save by your right hand those who take refuge in you from their foes."

NOVEMBER

After Action Report (AAR)

22

Countdown
DAY

23

Countdown
DAY

24

Countdown
DAY

25

Countdown
DAY

26

Countdown
DAY

27

Countdown
DAY

28

Countdown
DAY

NOVEMBER

Bible Update Brief

29

Psalm 5: 2: "Listen to my cry for help, my King and my God, for to you I pray."

30

Psalm 55: 22: "Cast your cares on the Lord and He will sustain you; He will never let the righteous fall."

NOVEMBER

After Action Report (AAR)

29

Countdown
DAY

30

Countdown
DAY

NOTES

NOTES

NOTES

WORDS OF ENCOURAGEMENT

(from an e-mail dated December 31, 2004)

Good morning Son,

You will be crossing into 2005 by the time you get this e-mail. Two thousand four will be a closed out year. This has been a year we will always remember, huh?

I am looking forward to the New Year and you coming home shortly. "Shortly," what a great word! I can already feel the pride welling up inside as I think about how we will watch you march on that field knowing you are home and the incredible job you did for our country and for the future freedom of an entire nation. I'll have to wear double-waterproof mascara for sure that day!

I know the hardest part of things is right before the end of a matter, so I want to encourage you to keep your eyes on the goal, your focus centered, your battle mindset sharp. The enemy will be fierce, but you will be stronger still in the Lord.

How I pray for you, my dear, fine soldier-son. I admire you and feel such pride. All the good seed in you has grown into such good fruit. Don't you ever focus on weeds of the past…they withered and died. God cleared the field, watered your life seeds, and they are evident for everyone to see.

Continue to let your humor bless your fellow soldiers and your duty and attitude be an inspiration. Don't focus on what is wrong…be part of all that is right! It is our foundation that makes us different, makes us have peace when everything around us is shaking…even when everything in us is shaking. There is still that peace that comes from the Prince of Peace who dwells in us.

We are salt and light because of the Light that shines in us and through us. Salt tastes best on things that are tasteless and it preserves things for generations. Light always overcomes darkness!

Be a standard this last portion of your time in Iraq, for God has raised His standard over your life. Dear Jesus, how I love you!! Stand strong and be courageous!

Your Warrior Mom

DECEMBER

Bible Update Brief

1

Psalm 93: 1: "The Lord reigns, He is robed in majesty; the Lord is robed in majesty and is armed with strength."

2

Psalm 30: 5: "For His anger lasts only a moment, but His favor lasts a lifetime; weeping may remain for a night, but rejoicing comes in the morning."

3

Psalm 25: 16: "Turn to me and be gracious to me, for I am lonely and afflicted."

4

Psalm 33: 20: "We wait in hope for the Lord; He is our help and our shield."

5

Psalm 61: 3: "For you have been my refuge, a strong tower against my foe."

6

Psalm 95: 1: "Come, let us sing for joy to the Lord; let us shout aloud to the Rock of our salvation."

7

PEARL HARBOR DAY

Psalm 17: 8: "Keep me as the apple of your eye; hide me in the shadow of your wings from the wicked who assail me, from my mortal enemies who surround me."

DECEMBER

After Action Report (AAR)

1

Countdown
DAY

2

Countdown
DAY

3

Countdown
DAY

4

Countdown
DAY

5

Countdown
DAY

6

Countdown
DAY

7

Countdown
DAY

DECEMBER

Bible Update Brief

8

Psalm 119: 122: "Ensure your servant's well-being; let not the arrogant oppress me."

9

Psalm 3: 7: "Arise, O Lord! Deliver me, O God! Strike all my enemies on the jaw; break the teeth of the wicked."

10

Psalm 31: 2: "Turn your ear to me, come quickly to my rescue; be my rock of refuge, a strong fortress to save me."

11

Psalm 92: 4: "For you make me glad by your deeds, O Lord; I sing for joy at the works of your hands."

12

Psalm 118: 24: "This is the day the Lord has made; let us rejoice and be glad in it."

13

Psalm 16: 1: "Keep me safe, O God, for in you I take refuge."

14

Psalm 111: 7-8: "The works of His hands are faithful and just; all His precepts are trustworthy. They are steadfast for ever and ever, done in faithfulness and uprightness."

DECEMBER

After Action Report (AAR)

8

Countdown
DAY

9

Countdown
DAY

10

Countdown
DAY

11

Countdown
DAY

12

Countdown
DAY

13

Countdown
DAY

14

Countdown
DAY

DECEMBER

Bible Update Brief

15

Psalm 57: 1b: "I will take refuge in the shadow of your wings until the disaster has passed."

16

Psalm 68: 20: "Our God is a God who saves; from the Sovereign Lord comes escape from death."

17

Psalm 85: 7: "Show us your unfailing love, O Lord, and grant us your salvation."

18

Psalm 92: 5: "How great are your works, O Lord, how profound your thoughts!"

19

Psalm 68: 3: "But may the righteous be glad and rejoice God; may they be happy and joyful."

20

Psalm 31: 7: "I will be glad and rejoice in your love, for you saw my affliction and knew the anguish of my soul."

21

Psalm 86: 12: "I will praise you, O Lord my God, with all my heart; I will glorify your name forever."

DECEMBER

After Action Report (AAR)

15
Countdown
DAY

16
Countdown
DAY

17
Countdown
DAY

18
Countdown
DAY

19
Countdown
DAY

20
Countdown
DAY

21
Countdown
DAY

DECEMBER

Bible Update Brief

22

Psalm 90: 1: "Lord, you have been our dwelling place throughout all generations."

23

Psalm 90: 2: "Before the mountains were born or you brought forth the earth and the world, from everlasting to everlasting you are God."

24

Psalm 86: 10: "For you are great and do marvelous deeds; you alone are good."

25

CHRISTMAS

Psalm 57: 1: "Have mercy on me, O God, have mercy on me, for in you my soul takes refuge."

26

Psalm 37: 40: "The Lord helps them and delivers them; He delivers them from the wicked and saves them, because they take refuge in Him."

27

Psalm 88: 1-2: "O Lord, the God who saves me, day and night I cry out before you. May my prayer come before you; turn your ear to my cry."

28

Psalm 30: 1: "I will exalt you, O Lord, for you lifted me out of the depths and did not let my enemies gloat over me."

DECEMBER

After Action Report (AAR)

22

Countdown
DAY

23

Countdown
DAY

24

Countdown
DAY

25

Countdown
DAY

26

Countdown
DAY

27

Countdown
DAY

28

Countdown
DAY

DECEMBER

Bible Update Brief

29

Psalm 40: 5: "Many, O Lord my God, are the wonders you have done. The things you planned for us no one can recount to you; were I to speak and tell of them, they would be too many to declare."

30

Psalm 118: 15: "Shouts of joy and victory resound in the tents of the righteous: 'The Lord's right hand has done mighty things!'"

31

Psalm 116: 6: "The Lord protects the simple hearted; when I was in great need, He saved me."

DECEMBER

After Action Report (AAR)

29

Countdown
DAY

30

Countdown
DAY

31

Countdown
DAY

NOTES

NOTES

NOTES

Made in the USA
Middletown, DE
04 December 2018